Eggy Hepburn has led a colourful and amusing life, spending childhood in Aldershot to later serving for 24 years in the Royal Navy. During his early life, a person who was supposed to protect and nurture him into adulthood abused him to such an extent that Eggy sought police assistance after 50 years of hiding it, which eventually ended in Crown Court.

Once the secret was revealed, all of his siblings and family stood by him as he slowly went downhill and spiralled into depression, especially as his mother passed away before the case in court.

He is now on the road to recovery, where there is light at the end of the tunnel, getting brighter each day and the love and support from family and friends is immeasurable.

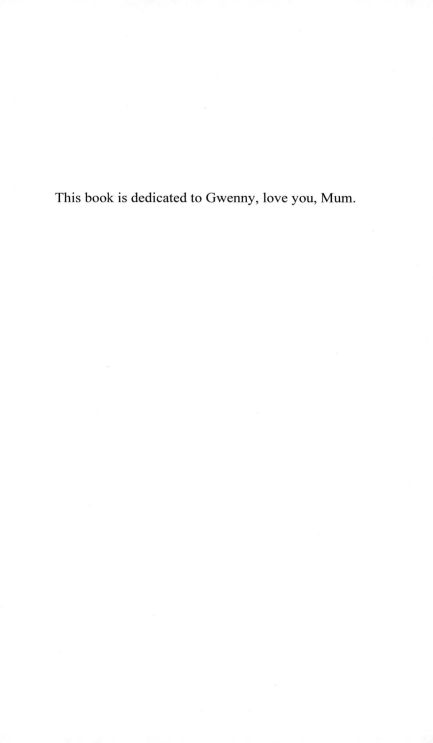

This book is dedicated to Gwenny, love you, Mum.

Eggy Hepburn

THE 50-YEAR SECRET

A Secret That Should Be Told

AUSTIN MACAULEY PUBLISHERS™

LONDON * CAMBRIDGE * NEW YORK * SHARJAH

A CIP catalogue record for this title is available from the British Library.

ISBN 9781398409125 (Paperback)
ISBN 9781398409132 (ePub e-book)

www.austinmacauley.com

First Published (2021)
Austin Macauley Publishers Ltd
25 Canada Square
Canary Wharf
London
E14 5LQ

My heartfelt thanks to my wife and children for all of their help in getting me through the dark times.

My thanks to my stepdad, Steve, who has been my father since joining the family all those years ago.

Thanks to my four sisters who finally understood why I never had a relationship with my biological male adult. Thanks to Sean and Jason at Surrey Police in Guildford SIU. Thanks to the Crown Prosecution Service.

Many thanks to the Royal Navy for the use of the pictures in accordance with the UK Ministry of Defence © Crown copyright (1975 - 1986). Thanks also to Austin Macauley for believing in this book and making it a reality.

This is a true story of something I have kept hidden from my family for 50 years. It is about a subject that is quite prevalent these days and it is about an event in my life that did happen and has ended up in Crown Court.

I have decided to tell the story of my life as there must be others who have been in the same situation and, like me, have not said anything. Everything you read is true, there is no need to lie or fabricate anything. I hope you discover that there are no winners or losers and find a lot of laughter but also sorrow and sadness as I reveal the secret.

As it involves my family, I have changed their names.

My name is Eggy. You might ask...an odd name? This nickname was given to me by a school friend and neighbour when I was about six years old and I have always been known by that name and I had it changed by Deed Poll!!! As in all things in life, you cannot change your birth certificate but every other document (passport, driving licence, bank details etc.) can be. ☺

Quite handy for me as there must be one Eggy Hepburn so going through passport control is a breeze with the odd 'an unusual name' from the officer.

I was born in Aldershot in 1958 to Gwendoline and Brian with one older and three younger sisters. Anne (1956) is the eldest then Jane (1960), Susan (1962) and Dawn (1966). My first memory is that of a 3 or 4-year-old living in Winchester Road in Ash, with plenty of mums, brothers and sisters in the same street. One thing that has stayed in my memory bank from those days was we had an outside loo and I'm sure there was a cesspit at the bottom of the garden.

I have a small scar below my left eye and as the years go by you learn how things like this happen. I don't know which way around but Anne tells me she stabbed me with a pencil because I threw her hamster on the fire. Next we moved to Denmark Street in Aldershot and I remember walking to my first school with Anne and we used to pass our nan's house (Brian's mum) on the way. Some days she would be in the garden for a quick hello on the way. We did not have a lot of money in those days, so I had to wear shorts and those plastic shoes which I think are called Jellies these days and they didn't last five minutes.

Denmark Street is where I have awful memories of certain foods which I still hate to this day. Rice pudding, tapioca, marmalade and worst of all fat on meat. Even thinking about the fat makes my stomach gurgle. Again, as money was tight, we had to eat everything that was put in front of us and I couldn't leave the table until it was all eaten.

We didn't live too long in that street because my next memory is that of Manfield Road (1963) in Ash and again walking to the primary school with Anne and wearing those awful plastic shoes.

I had also graduated to long trousers but always came home with the knee section missing and a gravel rash. I have some great memories of going to primary school which in today's climate and political correctness would not have happened. One of the kids (Mike) had been given a boomerang as a gift and I remember going on to the school field with him so we could try out this curved piece of wood. There were three kids on the field and I was next to Mike as he pulled back his arm and gave the boomerang an almighty throw into the sky (not bad for a 6-year-old) and we watched in awe as it started to climb as it went out in a large circle and start to return. Obviously as something goes up it must come down and it did…smack on top of the other kid's head. All that open space and he managed to hit this other kid! We couldn't even throw it away as it kept coming back. We did take the other kid to the school reception for treatment to the cut.

I'll let you all know now that I was not an angel as a kid or in fact a model student when it came to lessons in school. I was one of those kids that couldn't sit still or take in what was being taught and was always being told off. One boy (Martin) and I were doing something during a lesson and he was called up to the teacher's desk and for whatever reason he was told to sit on the floor next to the desk which he did under protest, the teacher then tried to push him under the desk and at the same time bashed his head on the corner of the desk…another trip to reception.

I remember going to school and being told to be careful when entering and leaving the school grounds as a girl had lost her middle finger when the large metal gate was accidently closed on her hand. It's funny how you would avoid that gate and give it a wide berth.

Everyone hates school dinners? I don't know why but at primary school, I was always up first to get a second helping. This is because money was tight at home and as before I never ate what was on the table at home until I was force fed. ☺

Sunday school is another place that I used to go to…again not for long. Mum gave us some coppers (these are money before decimalisation farthing, halfpenny and penny) which we would put on a collection plate which came around at the end of the morning lessons. Now me being me noticed that a nice big half crown (25p) was staring at me so when I put my coppers in, I tried to remove it but got caught. Here ended the Sunday school trips.

Manfield road was full of all types of people as probably most streets are these days. John who lived opposite our house has been and still remains a friend since meeting and has the dubious honour of giving me my nickname. As kids we did everything together, good and bad. We would spend a lot of time away from home (you will hear another reason later) as we grew up by this, I mean out as soon as possible leave in the morning and coming back in the evening playing as kids do. Walking for miles, well it seemed like miles as I had little legs and getting up to mischief. One occasion there were about five of us wandering around Ash and saw a large open sided barn about half full of bales of straw which we inhabited for an afternoon. Stacking the bales as high as we could to build a den and having a laugh. Next thing that happens is the bales start to fall in and this elderly gentleman starts ranting at us and lashing out with a length of string with a knot in the end. Three of us were hit and the old bill arrived to transport us home. Once in the house we were sat down and given the lecture about damaged to property by the police and then the obligatory bollocking from my mum and sent to bed. At the top of the stairs on the way up to bed was a window and I could see out of it that two of the lads were being dragged down their garden-path both screaming and getting a clip around the ears by their mum. It was at this point as my mum was about to come up the stairs that I said what the farmer had hit us with and I pointed out to her the rather large red welt on my leg.

Mum went ballistic and off she went to tell the copper and farmer and I had to show the mark on my leg, at this point no further action was taken. It was later that day that I found out that the other two boys did not show their mark because their mum had given them such a beating as they couldn't decide which marks the farmer had made.

Growing up in Ash was fun as a child and I have great memories during this period. I had a couple of jobs one of which was going on an ice cream van (Mylo) for a couple of hours helping serve and learn how to do a cone like Mr Whippy…more on the floor than the cone. We headed off from one street to the next and I sat in the back by the ice cream dispenser as there was no seat on the passenger side and as we turned a corner a bit too sharp the draw till came flying out with cash going everywhere. As Mylo was driving and looking over his shoulder at all the coins on the floor, I started to pick the money up and put the draw back in the slot. He was watching me like a hawk but I still managed to come away with four half crowns (£1) in my socks.

The second job was a milk round (Jim) on the weekends and I'd get up at stupid o'clock in the morning and walk from Ash to Aldershot (about two miles) and either get to the dairy or Jim would pick me up in the three-wheel electric milk float. This round would take about five hours and I would get a couple of quid for it. I got told off one day for driving the float along the road and Jim went nuts at me because I had made him walk about 100 meters. I can still remember the milk round route that we covered to this day.

Another school friend lived in a pub called The King's Head in Ash and as we were both naughty boys getting up to mischief, he decided to go in to the pub and pinch some cash. He came out with two of those coin bags you get from banks which were full of sixpence pieces (2.5p) and 40 number 6 cigarettes, so we spent the day in Guildford living it up like a pair of rich kids eating what we could and smoking like it was going out of fashion. Another pub nearby was The Bricklayers Arms and I used to jump over the fence beside the pub and pinch a couple of Brown Ale empty beer bottles and then take them back in to the off-licence part of the pub to get the money back and buy sweets. This bottle return system is making a comeback and is now called recycling.

Not far from The King's Head was an old disused railway line which is where I learnt how to drive a motor bike. I can't remember who I was with at the time but the bike was an Ariel Square 4 and a big old lump of a beast. The bike was kick-started to get it fired up and off I went in a straight line but trying to turn it on an old railway line was difficult to say the least. To stop it I had to put my hand down and cover what I now know to be is the air inlet for the carburettor which is what I did. Turned it around as best as I could as I was some distance from where I started from and attempted to kick-start it. I failed miserably at that and had to walk back to where I started from.

Up until the age of 11, I can honestly say that I was a naughty boy and have memories of my biological father being an absolute twat of a man and a bully towards me. I will always refer to him as my biological father because that is all he is. I was mentally, physically and sexually abused by him and the latter I will tell you about later. My mum and sisters have always asked me why I have never had a relationship with him throughout my life but now they understand why.

My sister, Anne, had her 50th birthday party and a cake was made with a picture on it of us as a family as kids and she wanted to recreate the picture at the party...I declined. I think my mum and sisters had inkling later on in life as to why I hated him so much but I never said anything. As a child I was always getting a beating from him, okay I was naughty, and in those days, this was the norm. One day sitting in the front room opposite him while he had his dinner on a tray, he picked up a china cup which was empty of tea and threw the cup which hit me in the stomach. Still I'm none the wiser why.

We had gas and electric-meter under the stairs and I had learnt how to pick the lock on the electric one with a hair clip and take some of the coins. My parents used to wonder why it was always short of money when the meter-man came to collect.

Next it was on to Yeoman's Bridge Secondary School which had a headmaster who nobody liked and was feared by all. On day one as a first-year new boy walking around and being excited I accidently bumped into a fifth year who decided to be big in front of his mates giving it large by a bit of pushing and invite me to meet him by the bottom gate after school. Unknown to me, this was the meeting place if you had any grievances that needed settling. As I said it was an accident, so I took up his offer and duly met him after school. A large crowd was gathered and as I made my way towards him, the crowd opened and then closed behind me. I do remember that he ended up on the floor with a bloody nose and I went home without a scratch.

Again, at secondary school, I was not one for learning at the beginning and got bored during lessons. Art was one of these occasions when I came across a small bottle of Indian ink and a pin. I left the lesson with six self-made tattoos on my right hand and one on my left. Gives it away that I'm left-handed. I had Eggy on my right forearm, E H between the thumb and forefinger, dots on the knuckles and E H on two of the fingers. On the left I had dots by the thumb.

I had a couple of punch-ups at Yeoman's Bridge and one was with a friend. I saw him many years ago and we are still undecided as to why it started but he always reminds me that he ended up with half a tooth missing. Don't get me wrong, I was not a bully and only had a fight to defend myself but you do learn from your mistakes. A craze going around the school was putting a load of elastic bands together to make them about 18 inches long then folding bits of paper nice and small, wrapping it around the elastic and launching the paper at people. These stung like mad when they hit. I crept up to a lad called Michael in the playground and fired one in his ear from about two feet and he unsurprisingly cried out in pain so I left the scene. A couple of minutes later a lad came up to me and said, "Dan wants to see you in the cloak room." So off I went, entered the room and walked to the end but it was empty and as I turned around to go back out, I got a whack in the face and this lad over me saying, to don't do that again to Michael. I didn't do it again to anyone.

My school reports didn't make for good reading either. I had plenty of bad remarks from teachers and unnecessary comments from the twat. I wish I could get a copy of this report and did try a long time ago but was unsuccessful. The school has changed name since I left in 74 and they didn't have digital then. The first computer I ever saw was in the maths class room and was half the size of the room. I think it took two days to warm it up.

A week or so before leaving school, me and John heard that the teachers had a bit of a shindig one night and the left-over booze was in the PT store. So off we went and using a metal comb we opened the store and found a couple of bottles of white wine. Great! Party time. Only problem was that we didn't have a corkscrew so we smashed the top of the bottle and sat there drinking. After leaving the PT store, a bit worse for wear, we were told to go to the main hall as a special assembly had been organised and what I didn't know was I was due to receive something… It was during the assembly that I was removed from the hall as I had fallen asleep and was snoring. Something to do with the alcohol…maybe.

Aldershot is home to the British Army and during the '70s while I was at school, we all heard a rumble and later found out that day, the IRA had car bombed the HQ of the Parachute Regiment as a revenge for the Bloody Sunday incident.

In 1974, I left school and joined the Royal Navy. The main reason for this was to get out of the house. I had arranged it all by myself but at some stage the twat must have had to sign something for me to go as I was 16. This was one of the best decisions I have ever made in my life and I have no regrets. I had all the paperwork sent to me and had instructions to go to London for a full medical which I did all on my own! I was 16, getting a train from Aldershot to London then walking the streets looking for the Careers Office in

Southampton Row. I had an interview and then a medical which was the first time I had to cough in front of a doctor. ☺

If I can give one piece of advice to youngsters these days is join one of the services simply because you will be paid, fed, watered and have a roof over your head as long as you can. I spent 24 years travelling the world.

As with all the armed forces you have to do the basic training first and this is where they break you down and then build you up to learn the discipline that you need in a service environment. I started my career at HMS Raleigh in Torpoint and learning the basics of bulling shoes, ironing and washing your own clothes with the obligatory, "Yes sir, no sir, three bags full, sir." Kit muster was a nightmare! You had to make your bed and using the counter pain as a guide (folded with three diamonds showing at the top and four at the bottom) lay your kit out in such a way that it was all nice and straight on your bed. Boots and shoes were on the floor at the end of the bed shining so you could see your face in them. As space on a warship was minimum, everything was folded neatly and to a certain size, with this in mind you were issued a pay book which had written inside any kit issued to you long term, things like your gas mask. This book is about 3 x 4 inches and was used to measure the creases in your number 1 and number 2 uniform trousers. Number 1 was your best uniform with gold badges and number 2 was with red badges. As I say we had to put creases in the trousers and these went horizontal and opposite so that you could fold the trousers up like a concertina. Depending on your height, you had either five or seven creases, I had seven and you used the pay book to govern the distance between the horizontal creases turning over each leg so the folds were opposite each other. Sailors have it easy these days as the crease is vertical and hung in wardrobes.

Going home on leave was a bit daunting as I had to travel in full uniform from Plymouth to Aldershot then walk half a mile to the house. It was a bit later that you were allowed to travel in civvies as you were deemed a target.

After HMS Raleigh, I went to HMS Vernon in Portsmouth and trained how to become a TAS Ape, Torpedo and antisubmarine operator learning how to use the ship's sonar. Again as we were under training so still had the bullshit of kit muster and be somewhere at a certain time but had a bit more freedom to leave the base and learn the art of drinking alcohol. I also had my first proper tattoo done under the arches outside the gate of Vernon. Once training was finished, we had to select where we would like to serve in the fleet and what class of ship, so I opted for a Portsmouth-based Leander-class frigate, no chance there as I ended up with a Rosyth-based Tribal-class frigate, HMS Nubian. I travelled up with three others from Vernon joining the ship on the same day and was quite happy on arrival as we were told the ship is off to Gibraltar, Malta and then nine months in the West Indies! That is where 1975 disappeared. In the navy when you are posted anywhere it is called a draft and my next one from Nubian was to HMS Nelson in Portsmouth in 1977 to wait my next sea draft. I worked on the Commander-in-Chief's barge which was called a green parrot and this was berthed in the dockyard. I was one of those sailors that stood on the bow or stern with a boat hook for ceremonial duties and for coming alongside. What we used to call a cushy number as I also lived in C-in-C house in the dockyard as well. I had a good oppo (friend) who called one day for a couple of beers so we went into Pompey to the Mucky Duck, Yorkshire Grey and Might Fine to name a few and got three sheets to the wind. One of these pubs had a barrel on the bar in which you could dip your glass (with a handle) in and get a pint of cloudy liquid with pips and bits of apple (scrumpy) which tasted awful until you had three or four of them. We had an altercation with a fella in a pub and took him outside to show him the error of his ways…mistake as we were both arrested by the old bill and ended up in court charged with GBH. I was also dismissed from the barge crew and returned to Nelson. In court we were found guilty and fined £100 with £100 costs which was a lot of money then. The only beef I have with the case is that they found us guilty without the victim turning up in court and no witnesses. I also got punished by the Navy, by that I mean as I spent 3.5 days in court, so I had an extra 3.5 days added to my service. It was while I was at Nelson that I met my wife, Debby. She was in Pompey on a weekend visit and had come to Nelson to meet another sailor but she met this tall handsome rugged bloke instead. We met on a Monday, I moved in on the Tuesday and I asked to marry her on the Wednesday… We got married six weeks later and have been together to this day. 42 years so far. Our first married quarter was Rowner in Gosport and it was a 2-bed ground floor flat. On one occasion we were in bed and were woken by a strange noise…like heavy breathing at the end of the bed, it was two firemen in breathing apparatus asking us to leave the flat as someone had noticed smoke billowing from the flat. We had an open fire in the front room which caused all the smoke.

Our first son, Jaimie, was born in 1979 in Portsmouth and I must be the only man to turn up in to a maternity ward bleeding from a head wound. I was walking to St Marys and didn't notice the road sign until after I head-butted it. ☺

I was then drafted to HMS Arethusa which was a Plymouth based IKARA Leander-class frigate which meant that the ship had a missile system that could launch a torpedo at a greater distance and had a Variable Depth Sonar (VDS) on the back end. When Jaimie was six weeks old, the ship sailed for a 9- month deployment to the Far East, so he was 11 months old when I came back. Jaimie was very ill as a baby and spent a lot of time in and out of hospital having test after test to see what was wrong to no avail. Deb did all the appointments and when I came back from the Far East, he had spent time in hospitals in London because of his bad chest. We were sent to the Royal Naval Hospital Haslar in Gosport for a new test and he was made to breath a mixture which then drew a picture on the screen, it was at this point I noticed the screen only showed a picture of his right lung, next thing we know we are under the care of Great Ormond Street Hospital undergoing more tests which is eventually diagnosed as MacLeod's Syndrome. We then moved to married quarters in Hendon as it was easier to get to and from GOSH. J did go to theatres for removal of what remained of the lung but they were unable to do the procedure as they could not get a camera into the lung. In 1980 our daughter Jemma was born while I was still on Arethusa which was in Plymouth at the time, Debs family are all from the East End of London so when I got the call that J had been born, I grabbed a case of beer and a bunch of flowers and boarded the train from Plymouth to London. Deb tells me that I arrived at the hospital in Mile End with half a bunch of stalks wrapped in paper and four cans of beer.

Apparently, my breath smelled lovely as I had eaten the flowers on the way up.

In 1982 our son, Mitchell, was born and I was serving with the Royal Navy Display Team touring the UK doing the Window Ladder and Mast Manning. This was the year of the Falklands Campaign so the Navy were headline news. As always, I got up to mischief and we toured in a big bus around the country to events like the Royal Bath and West Show, East of England show and smaller venues. One of these places I decided to take a few of the lads on a trip around an RAF base we were staying on by pinching the tour bus. Another bollocking heading in my direction. We did stay in some decent hotels and had everything paid for but as we were all doing a lot of fitness, alcohol was frowned upon. One of the senior officers had brought his wife to one of the hotels for the weekend and we had a good laugh with them. I managed to waffle to the reception that we needed access to his executive suite as he had left something behind and six of us entered the room and promptly moved the bed and most of the contents of his room into the bathroom. I don't know if I have something written on my forehead but at breakfast the next morning, I could see him making a bee line to me with his wife in tow and he had steam coming out of his ears. As they both approached me, his wife burst into laughter and said it was the funniest thing that she had seen. He did eventually calm down and later used that incident as an anecdote. The best time during the RNDT tour was the Festival of Remembrance at the Royal Albert Hall. If you have never seen the window ladder basically it is four large frames with 16 small squares in each which are then suspended about 40 feet off the ground supported by large wooden poles all held up by blocks and tackles weighing a ton each and all of which is carried into the arena and erected by hand, two frames to the left, two to the right at slight angles to each other. The display is then carried out to music where 16 men in Red on one side and 16 in Blue on the other stand under the frame. We climb a rope (four shifts) and enter the frame, climb to the top until all 32 are seated then do a routine again to music before exiting the frames back down the rope. Now in the Royal Albert Hall it is impossible to walk in with the gear and erect it so it is suspended on wires and is higher than what we were used to. It takes five shifts to get in. The other problem was that there were no supports so when the routine was in full swing so were the four frames from one side of the hall to the other!!! I also performed in front of the Royal Family and lots of me on TV when it was televised as I'm photogenic…not. Two other times which I enjoyed was being the button boy when we did the Mast Manning. This again was set to music so by the time it was finished, I stood on the top of a 90-foot mast on a dinner plate (the button) holding on to a lightning conductor. What goes up must come down so music again and the team would descend, it's at this point that you hold on for dear life as everyone starts moving and the mast shakes and I mean shakes!!! As most of the team dismount the mast, I have to turn sideways and begin the climb down the mast and stand on a ladder with my eye level on the button. Next, I grab a rope (and hold it very tightly) which is anchored below the button and begin hand over hand down the rope to the floor. This rope is at about a 35-degree angle so you don't rush it. What I did forget on my first climb down was to wear climbing tights (the ones we wore during the window ladder display) under my white trousers so as I climb down hand over hand and my legs wrapped around the rope, my trousers began to ride up so when I came off the rope near the bottom and run to the centre of where all the team are gathered to receive my gift for carrying out such a daring feat (a poxy glass tankard at the Aldershot Army Show) my leg begins to sting. We got back to the debrief area and lifted the trouser leg up and what did we see…a massive friction-burn from my ankle to the top of my calf looking like the map of Africa. I was grounded for two weeks to wait for it to heal. The next time I was a button boy was at the Henry Cooper Walkabout in the White City Stadium in London. Same routine, but with the added climbing tights on this time. Off the mast, I ran to the centre, salute and was presented with a crystal decanter (still got it!) by the lovely Joanna Lumley. Had to give this lovely lady a peck on the cheek when receiving the decanter…I got a bollocking off the Mrs for that.

1983 I was drafted to the aircraft carrier HMS Invincible which was one of the ships in the Task Force and as it had returned from the Falkland Islands, most of the crew were changed. I spent three years as part of her crew and sailed to the Far East and the USA. Part of my duties on board was as QM (Quartermaster) this was driving the ship when at sea and manning the gangway when in harbour controlling access to the ship and carry out ceremonial duties. During the Far East trip (about half way), some of our families flew out to Sydney to meet up with us and have a well-earned holiday. As the ship had sailed a couple of days before our holiday had finished and we said goodbye to our loved ones for their return home, we were transported to an airbase near Sydney and flown to Melbourne by Hercules (long flight sitting on cargo netting) to an Aussie RAF base and on arrival a couple of Sea King

Helicopters from the ship were waiting for us for the next leg to return to Invincible. As we touched down on board and allowed off the chopper, one of the Medics came up to me and said you are needed in the sickbay (Medical Centre) so off I went. Once inside the doc says welcome back, hope you had a nice time in Sydney it's now time for your Vasectomy!!! Wow…that was painful, not what he said but the actual operation as I felt myself sliding down the table as he pulled things about. After a couple of days, I used to leave 20 mins before anyone else as it took me that long to get to the dining hall in the middle of the ship trying to walk with what felt and looked like a couple of cricket balls between my legs. Two weeks later I had all the tattoos removed from my hands as the surgeon on board was a specialist in plastic surgery. ☺ Part of my duty as a QM was to make announcements over the loudspeaker system and to check the ship on occasions (rounds); I also had an assistant who was known as the Bosun's Mate who also carried out tasks. I remember him coming back from our mess (5 Echo Starboard) and saying to me, I had better get down to the mess asap. I got to the mess and opened the door but it was pitch black, I switched on the lights and there were two lads humping the life out of a blow-up doll…one in each end. I gave them their marching orders and said, I'll be back in five minutes as the pair were using Vegemite as a lubricant! Not a pretty picture. I returned as the doll was deflating on the floor and the lads cleaning themselves.

Two more events that I could have been in big trouble for while on Invincible were that the mess entrance (5ES) was on a cross passage at the front of the ship and regularly someone would knock the door and leg it. Knock down ginger I called as a kid. Anyway one time there was a knock, so I open the door, nobody there, so I shut the door. As I'm about to sit down again the door opens and in comes Daz (mess mate) with a lad from another mess, I ask what he wants and Daz says I just caught this lad running around the corner and trying to hide. At last the culprit is apprehended. I dish out the justice by using a roll of HBM (2-inch-wide Harry Black Masking Tape) and taped his hands to his head and send him packing. After about 20 mins of laughter in our mess, I hear a broadcast for me to attend the Chief of Police Office (Master at Arms) and as I enter and look on a table there is what looked like a half a football but the insides were hairy, an inverted cat. The culprits mess mates had to cut the tape from his head...and another bollocking.

The last one was about the NAAFI canteen assistant who lived in our mess and was a civvy. This lad was a bit of a gobshite and rubbed people up the wrong way. One evening after coming off watch about midnight, he was in the mess giving it large again with alcohol in his system so I asked him politely to go to his bunk and sleep it off. After a few minutes of asking, he started getting louder so I said if he didn't go to bed, I would put him to bed...which I did with a left hook. Next morning the number 2 in the police department corners met in the passage outside the Police Office and asks which hand I hit him with, "Don't know what you are on about, John." After a bit of denying it, I get the last chance so I say, "This one."

John takes it and shakes it saying, "It's about time someone gave him a clip." Phew no bollocking this time. I had a great time on Invincible but a bit of a mechanical problem we had was that during the Far East trip, we had an issue with one of the propellers, you could stand on the Quarter deck which is under the flight deck at the rear of the ship and bounce up and down so we went into Singapore to have one of the bearings changed in one of the two mounts that support the prop. There is an A bracket (as it looked like an upside-down A) and a P bracket (you get the picture) they put the ship in dry dock and change the A bracket bearing. Couple of days later sea trials and we have the same problem, off we go back into Singapore dry dock and change the bearing in the P bracket off to sea again for trials and…yes same problem, back into dry dock. Eventually they find out we have an egg-shaped prop shaft and they can't repair it so we have to miss out on Hong Kong and Japan to return to the UK. Great, you might say except that we had to come back on one prop and as one of the drivers of this 20000-ton warship the midship position for the rudders was 10 degrees to Port.

After leaving Invincible, I was drafted to HMS Warrior in Northwood London which was the NATO Headquarters and run from underground. I moved the family to married quarters in Watford as again it was easier to get to and from GOSH for appointments. While I was at warrior, I asked the drafting team if there was any possibility of a draft to HMS Rooke in Gibraltar and with help from GOSH saying that the climate would be beneficial for Jaimie, I was posted there for two and a half years. I managed to get an extension when there and ended up doing three years one month and six days. Not that I counted. What a draft though, I spent two years working for the British Forces Broadcasting Service in the evenings and weekends as a DJ. I spent more time there than at work and I also got paid for DJing. Gib was the best draft I ever had as my family were with me for the whole time. We spent most weekends in Spain as the resorts of Estepona, Marbella, and Torremolenos and Malaga were all in easy reach by car. Shopping in Gib for tourism is excellent but if you live there, then the easiest thing to do was again cross the border and drive to the Continente which was like a hypermarket and get all your needs. We even drove to the Algarve on a couple of occasions to have annual leave. One day in Gib the Mrs sent me out to the shops for some items but I got a bit misdirected and returned with a big red W tattooed on each of my bum cheeks. I have had a few comments on, "Why do you have WW on your arse…" An explanation of "When I bend over, what does it say"? WoW. ☺ I have seen some really funny tattoos. I saw one morning that a sailor was shaving his chest from bottom right to top left…odd? When he turned around, I could see he had a Lawnmower Tattooed on the top of his shoulder.

Whilst in Gib, Deb worked in Rooke Junior Rates bar for a while and got to know a group of Royal Marines and a couple of American Servicemen. It was later down the line that we learnt they were SBS and members of the US SEAL Teams on exercise. One of the Marines became a regular visitor to our house in Gib and on return to the UK. We had some great times with this bunch!!! One morning my daughter was up early and came into our bedroom saying, "Dad…There's some men in black in the front room."

I get up and six SBS/SEAL fellas were all over the front room in the chairs and on the floor. I saw my mate and said, "How the fuck did you get in here?" He told me that they had parachuted in during the night and as my place was the closest, they decided to break in over the balcony and sleep in my place. Lucky for them I lived on the ground floor.

It was while in Gib that I decided to transfer to the Regulating Branch (Service Police) and passed a two-week assessment working with them on patrol. The main area of patrol was Main Street and when the RN Warships came for a visit, it was a case of picking up the drunken sailors/ Royal Marines and returning them to their ships with no further action. It was a different story if you managed to get arrested by the local police as we would have to collect you from the cells and return you to your ship with a report from the old bill. After leaving Gib, I was drafted to the Royal Naval Hospital Haslar in Gosport and worked as an armed sentry on the main entrance doing shift work around the clock until my Reg Course. I did see some sights! One that sticks in my mind is that a car going a bit faster than normal came up to the barrier with two people in the front so as I bent down to talk to the driver and he franticly explained that he had to get to A and E as quick as possible as his passenger was bleeding heavily. I looked across and noticed this lad was sitting on a black bin liner (well...Red and Black now) holding his crotch. I asked what was up and he took his hand away to reveal he had caught his foreskin in his jeans!!! Directions to A and E given and the barrier was raised. Next I was sent to the Reg School in Whale Island (HMS Excellent) where I learnt to be a military policeman. Lots of classroom work and exams to learn about the police and Criminal Evidence Act (1984) and interviewing techniques with 14 others in the class. After completing the course, I was drafted to the Provost HQ in Portsmouth where again you are under assessment to learn vehicle patrols and any other duties as a new policeman. Normal patrol duties in a caged van in police livery around Pompey and working closely with the Civilian Police, again depending on the severity of the case (drunk, fighting pissing in doorways) if sailors were arrested by the police, then they would hand them over to be dealt with by Naval Authorities. This would mean that the sailor/Marine would present in front of the commanding officer and be punished with naval regulations: stoppage of leave, extra work periods etc.

One of the funniest events that happened while on patrol in Portsmouth was with my great friend Fez, we were out on patrol and a call came over the radio to assist in the evacuation of patients at an MH hospital so we arrived, lead to a ward and started to help. Fez and I both helped a couple of elderly ladies from their beds and wrapped them in a blanket, put them in wheelchairs and took them to the evacuation meeting point on the hospital grounds in a car park. It was that stage when my little old lady started to lean forward, so I put a hand on her shoulder to stop her falling from the chair. As I was holding and pushing at the same time, she got much stronger and I was holding her back so I shouted to Fez, "Mate, we got a jumper trying to escape."

Fez looked at me, laughing his head off and said, "You have run over the blanket and it's caught around the wheel."

My next draft was to a tiny island in the middle of the Indian Ocean called Diego Garcia. This is a British Indian Ocean Territory leased to the USA. In other words, the Britishers owned it and the Yanks used it, so we had a British governor and the Island was policed by the Royal Navy, I was one of 12 Royal Overseas Police Officer (ROPO) number 1 being the Master at Arms and I was ROPO 12. Dog handler was ROPO 9. We also had a detachment of Royal Marines on the Island. We had a police station with a blue lamp outside and used American Police cars for patrols. Another draft considered as a good number, plenty of sunshine and great food and plenty of beer. While in DG, I decided to try for promotion and sat the exam for Regulating Petty Officer which I dually passed. I may not have got a promotion, later on down the line as an incident in DG could have scuppered that. I was called to a bar as an American had rather a skinful and was being noisy and obnoxious…once I had forcibly removed him from the bar and walked/staggered to the car, I managed to open the back door and literally threw him in onto the back seat and slammed the door. Unknown to me at this time one of his feet had caught in the hinge area but thankfully none of the toes were removed. I only knew I had done this was when we go back to the station and I open the door his leg drops out with a large bruise slowly appearing.

This is the chapter that I have had most difficulty talking about. I am more at ease writing it down but either way the memories come flooding back. I kept them buried for a long time and only told my wife after a few years of marriage as she wondered why I had no relationship with my biological father (Twat). I say it that way because I have no love or compassion for the twat and for what he did to me. There is no excuse. I can say that it really ruined my childhood and I have absolutely no respect for him. I for one will not attend his funeral… I just wish it was now. The court case was in June and I elected to appear by video link as I think my emotions might get the better of me and I would attack him as I can see all the lies coming out. Presumptuous I know but that is how I feel about it. Regardless of the outcome of the court case, the truth is 'I don't care'. If he goes to prison as an 80-year-old, so be it, if he gets found not guilty, then the system is shite because he DID abuse me.

As a child before and after the abuse started, I would spend as much time as possible out of the house. The twat was a bully and no matter what I did as a kid, it was wrong. I always had the feeling that I was not loved by him. The first sign of sexual abuse was when he asked me upstairs to have a bath. As a kid, I thought nothing of it and in the bath we were. It was later in life when you begin to understand about events in your life that turn it upside-down. While in the bath, I was aware that his foot was very close to me...I was basically sitting on it and it moved a lot. He also liked to wash my willie. Once out of the bath drying with a towel. I had a dry willie.

The same scenario on the second occasion with the bath routine but this time he had an erection and wanted me to hold it for him. I did not like what I saw or what he was doing and knew that it was wrong. What do I do? He is my father (Twat).

Same scenario for number 3 but after the bath it was into the main bedroom to complete the drying and showing me his erection with him masturbating and finishing in a hanky.

I always knew when this was going to happen as it was always a Thursday and Mum was at work. He would stand by the door until he got my attention and beckon me with his finger to follow him upstairs.

After the bath routine and into the bedroom, I knew something was different as he had pornographic magazines on the bed and asked me to turn around. He bent me forward and tried to penetrate me but I refused and clenched my buttocks and told him I didn't like it. He carried on rubbing himself between my legs while turning pages of the magazines until again he finished in a hanky. Thinking of it now this must have been the turning point as he never again touched me.

I felt and knew what he had done to me was wrong in so many ways but as an 11-year-old where could I turn to? Nobody would believe me. I swore to myself that if ever I had kids that they would never be subject to what I went through. To this day I can say 100% that my children or grandchildren have never seen my private parts. I always changed or got undressed where they could not see me.

My mum and sisters have always asked why I have never had a relationship with the twat, they know now of course. I am quite sure that he knew what he was doing and tried to groom me. He has never made contact with me or my family. No birthday, Christmas or anniversary cards for any of us.

I'm happy with that because in my mind he knows that I know he knows. I would have sent them back anyway.

A father is there to be a parent and guide you in life until you can do it on your own. Not this one, he is a bully, a liar, and worse of all a paedophile. How else can I describe a man who sexually abused his own son? The reason this all came out in the open was that I heard that some of my cousins had been abused. One of them was a family of eight kids and their father sexually abused one of the girls and also bullied some of the boys. I know she went to the police and reported it but the details she reported were lost. One of my cousins of the same family got wind of what he did and beat the shit out of him. Rough justice. One of my cousins from a different family daughter was also abused. They say that the abused becomes the abuser, maybe in his case but NOT in mine.

My mum and two of my sisters have been called as witnesses but I asked the CPS not to call Mum as she had been ill for about six months in 2018. In and out of hospital with a lung infection and then her skin started to appear to fall off.

This was diagnosed as Lupus, an incurable but treatable disease. She remained in Frimley Park Hospital until such time as she got better and was then transferred to Farnham Hospital because it was easier and closer for my stepdad (Steve) to visit. Steve visited Mum twice a day with Susan and her daughter in tow. Mum eventually seemed to get better but was bed bound and as I lived in Wales but worked in Germany, it was a bit difficult to see her as often as I would have liked. She was having regular physio as her legs were swollen like tree trunks and would cry when I phoned her as she was fed up being stuck in bed. You do what you can over the phone and tell her she needs to eat more so that her muscles can get better and she will be able to walk again. That advice fell on deaf ears. In fact, she was improving with her diet so much that it was decided to let her go home, so plans were put in place at the small flat to change the bedroom to the front room and a hoist put in to help her get in and out of bed. I made a group up on the WhatsApp and with my sisters we chatted every day about Mum and her progress and how upset she was about being stuck in bed and we all giving her the same advice about food, water, physio and going home. Tuesday 29 Jan, I had a message from Ann saying, they were transferring Mum back to Frimley Hospital for x-rays and tests but as she was going to the hospital, in the ambulance, she died. They did resuscitate her at the hospital but it didn't last long and she never came back. My personal opinion (and I'm not a doctor) is that she gave up. She was really unhappy about being stuck in bed and often said she did not want to be here. My wife and I flew back from Germany into Heathrow and drove to Aldershot to Susan's place and grieved with Steve, my sisters and their kids and started the ball rolling to make the funeral arrangements. Mum and Steve had a care plan in place so me and my sisters organised the flowers and the food for the wake all chipping in together. There is not a lot you can organise when a person dies until you have the death certificate and because Mum was an unexpected death the process is to go to the coroner to determine why she died. One week after Mum died, her sister, Gladys, passed away, another sad occasion.

We had to wait nearly a month for the death certificate and as a post-mortem was declined by Steve (I respect his decision). The coroner had to get all the information from those that gave treatment to Mum. Cause of death was: Aspiration Pneumonia, Depression with poor Oral Intake, Anti-Phospholipid Syndrome, Diverticulitis and Pulmonary Embolism. You will have to google that lot. ☺

The funeral was finally arranged for Friday, 15 March as her sister Glad was the week before. We didn't want Mum's brothers and sisters to attend two funerals in the same week, so it was arranged the week after.

We had the funeral at Aldershot Crematorium and filled the seats with plenty of people standing. Mum had her favourite songs by Daniel O'Donnell played and then it was my turn to say a few words. This is what I wrote and said:

I put this together for something to say
As this here place is only for one day
There comes a time when we say goodbye
Now Gwenny has gone to the place in the sky.

It is with sorrow that she has gone from us

But why did she always pinch me on the bus.

Our mum was a lady full of pride
Who loved to go out in the car for a ride.

50 was the limit when out in the car
But Bognor was a journey not too far.

Mum loved Butlins for many years.
She spent so much money on Gold Rush it ended in
tears.

Memories are there for all to hear
We all loved our mum very dear.

We have lost our mum who taught us to share
I was a naughty boy who didn't care.

We are a family without our leader
Especially as Gwenny was a force feeder.

As a boy she put food on the table
I wasn't allowed to leave until I was able
I still hate Marmalade, Rice pudding and fat
I'd feed the dog or slide it under the mat.

Mum liked a laugh and a joke
When the old man left, she found a decent bloke
Steve came in and settled down quick

I think he had to because she would give him a clip

Please don't sit there crying or having a fit
I'll still be known as Gwenny's little shit.

When the funeral had finished, the vicar said I had done two things that he never heard at a funeral…I had a round of applause and was the first person to swear. ☺

A few years ago, when my sisters and I were together at some occasion and we were just chewing the fat about when we were kids. The conversation turned to me always getting a beating from the twat for anything that I could get blamed for. This is when Jane decided to tell us that as kids at Christmas time when the chocolates were on the tree that she would pinch them, eat them then throw the wrappers under my bed!!! Got a few annual beatings from the twat and yes, I also pinched them lol.

I also told them this little story: when we were kids, we had the Beano comic delivered to our house and I was never first to read it as one of my sisters always got to it before me. One evening the day before the comic was due, I decided to put some drawing pins at the bottom of the stairs by the front door and went to bed. Next morning, I heard the letterbox rattle and shot down the stairs to grab the comic but ended up with drawing pins in the bottom of my feet!!! As I was moaning and groaning on the floor pulling the pins out, one of my sisters duly got the comic before me. My final draft in the navy was to HMS Dryad and spent 5 years in the Discipline Office leaving as a Regulating Petty Officer.

When I left the Navy in 1998, I found it difficult to adjust to civvy life having spent 24 years in a disciplined environment and coming to the big bad world. I had a course before leaving and learnt to drive JCBs. I had an HGV1 and a

PSV licence from the Navy and my first job was driving buses in and around Bridgend. Not a very satisfying job as the pay was crap! I was asked to do some overtime on my second day so I asked what the pay was…an extra 10p an hour!!! I never did any overtime. Next I drove container Lorries to and from Sony in Bridgend and also to and from Freightliner in Cardiff. I did a hobble one night (this is a cash in the hand job) and went to a depot in Lantrisant to pick up the cab and then connected it to a trailer. I was given the address which was Hellmans at Heathrow and off I went with no paperwork. I knew it was a heavy load as the slight inclines on the M4 tended to slow the lorry down. I arrived at the address and was directed to a loading bay and was asked if I came from the Royal Mint. Odd question so I said no. We opened up the side curtains of the trailer and there before my eyes were 16 pallets about 3 feet high with small boxes all sealed with Royal Mint straps containing about one Million Hong Kong Dollars in coins!!!

I chatted with the guy off loading and he said I was the third lorry up tonight and all of it was due out on a flight that night.

After lorry driving, I tried JCBs for a couple of months again not having any experience it was difficult to stay in this field of work. My next venture was to work in the cruise industry. Deb and I went to London for the interview which went well and they said we will let you know in a week or so. I was only down the road 10 minutes and was offered the job as a security officer!!!

I had a flight in a small jet from Cardiff to Paris then a long-haul flight to Chile where I met up with the Marco Polo and did four months up and down the east and west coast of

South America before crossing the pond to the Med where I left it for a two-month break. Next it was off to the crown Odyssey for four months going around and around the Med. A good life as the food was excellent and drink was provided but not to excess. I had a team of six Ghurkha's working for me doing the patrols and carrying out the security of the ships. When we were in port, I was always at the gangway area to oversee operations. I was also on-board at the time the Twin Towers were attacked, so security was increased, I am not saying that it was lacking in security but we did things with more interest. Bag searches, drug detection and bomb sniffing devices were more prevalent.

One of the cruises that was totally unforgettable was a gay cruise. On day one when all the passengers were due to embark my duty is in the reception area on the jetty where 900 people were waiting. (I remember that there were only two women). There was a family of four (two adults and two kids) looking a bit bewildered as there were all these men in different clothing (transvestite) and all other manner of gear. The family were taken to one side and given return flights home as their travel agent had made a big mistake. Generally the cruise was uneventful...well they were shagging in the Jacuzzi, shagging in the library in fact anywhere!!! I did the night patrols to keep an eye on things and was on the bridge one night looking down and saw a Daisy Chain...there were seven blokes in a line...I'll leave that up to your imagination. My reports to the Captain every morning were quite colourful.

My next job was with an Orthopaedic Manufacture and started in the picking and packing department despatching the Implants worldwide. I did this for about two years then I moved to the Marketing Services Department where I stayed for the next 12 years. My jobs were to set up and assist on Cadaveric courses throughout the Europe and also to build exhibition booths.

Cadavers are something you either like or can't handle…a bit like marmite. It's not everyone's cup of tea to see a dead body of a part of a body but it did not bother me. Yes, the smell sometimes can be overpowering (especially when you lift the legs up and it empties its bowels). Sometimes we had the bottom half of a body and would have to chisel out around the spine to put a clamp on it so that we could turn the lower half on its side to do hip replacement. One occasion we had just finished doing the knees on a body when the Lab Professor came in and said we had to send the body below as the family had turned up to view!!! Little did they know he had two new knees. Another time I was assisting a professor and we were doing the shoulder. Now this professor was very vocal and sometimes impatient and we were doing the Op to camera so the course participants could see in another room how it was done. I was holding the arm so he could show the shoulder anatomy and asked for a hammer…all eyes on the table and no one could see the hammer. "Where's the bloody hammer?" he bellowed, at this point I spotted it under some other instruments on the table and as I was holding the arm, I used it and manipulated the arm to actually touch the hammer. This did bring a smile to his face. For 10 years, I went to Vienna 14 times a year, Barcelona 8 times a year, Rotterdam six times a year and a few other places thrown in for good measure. We all managed to get to Platinum Card holder at some stage with KLM.

The courses are all attended by surgeons to practice how to put one of the company's products in as all companies' products or devices differ (even though they look the same). My thoughts are that if they make a mistake on these courses, then they won't make the same mistake on a live patient. This does not always work as I saw one surgeon put a left knee implant into a right knee and another hurt his wrist as he was trying to put a rasp that was three sizes to big down a femur.

We built exhibition booths all over Europe, some small (3m x 3m) and some large (10m x 10m) for the big events. We would take the whole booth (floor, floor covering, walls, graphics, TVs, Implant Models, etc etc) and build it a day or two before the event then go in after and dismantle the lot, put it on a lorry and get ready for the next one.

2015 was the year that I decided to talk to the police about events in my life as a kid and also started the slow downward spiral into depression and even contemplated ending it all. I had medical advice and was prescribed antidepressants. I struggled to sleep (still do to this day) zoned out and cried a lot because all I could see in my head was the abuse I suffered. Once it all came out in the open, the worst time was when I had to tell my mum what had happened and she did say that she knew something was not right with me and the twat and could only guess. Once she knew the truth, she understood.

It was also a tough time explaining to my children about my childhood abuse. They all knew that I did not have a relationship with him as they have never had any contact with him. After I had reported the abuse to the police, I was told by my sister (Dawn) that her daughter (C) had also been abused by the twat!!! She had been in and out of hospital as she kept having some fitting episodes and the doctors could not understand why and suggested therapy of some kind. After a couple of sessions, it became apparent that she was suffering with some type of PTSD and she has had some kind of trauma. It was at this stage that she revealed that she had been abused by her grandfather in a shed! When Dawn told me this, I said to her to report it to the police. Once all the information was gathered, the police decided to interview him and then charged the twat with 11 charges for both of us (6 for me and 5 for C).

When he was interviewed for me, he did a 'no comment' throughout but denied any wrongdoing when spoken to about C. He was sent to Magistrate Court and pleaded not guilty to all charges so was subsequently sent to Crown Court.

At the end of 2015, I took a redundancy package from the company and decided to retire at 57. We bought a static caravan in Pendine Sands and spent most of our time relaxing and getting away from it all. Don't get me wrong, I wasn't running away but wanted time on my own to get my head around the whole situation. After about 18 months, I got fed up being retired and decided to go back to work and worked in a private hospital as a porter for about a year and then worked for a company that transported young offenders (under 16) to and from court and secure units throughout the UK. The company also had a couple of houses that were used to house some of the young offenders before and after court and we babysat them 24 hours a day (12-hour shift). Some of these kids were brought up the wrong side of the law and were always in and out of trouble. They all had a chip on their shoulder and think that the world owes them everything. Some of them have really had a rough upbringing though. We also transported MH patients young and old to and from secure units.

One of the boys decided it would be fun to pull off a toilet cistern lid and throw it through a window. He also stole the credit card we used for fuel and tried to get cash out after legging it from the house. He was found later that day. These youngsters are also well aware of what they can and can't do but always want to push the boundaries. If they were under a court order, then you were able to use force to restrain then if the situation dictated. I used this once when we were transferring a 15-year-old from Cardiff to Northumberland. When in a van (it had three forward and one rear facing seats, separated from the driver with a TV and Xbox), there is the driver and two others in the rear (female staff for girls) and we would stop for toilet breaks and supply food when required (good behaviour warranted a MacDonald's!). When we were re-fuelling, this lad decided to get gobby to the staff opposite me and was about to spit at him so they had a little wrestling match and I grabbed his hand and put him in a goose neck hold, this had the desired effect as it is instant pain in the wrist and I had complete control of him. After sitting him down and calling us all the names under the sun, he apologised and said all he wanted was a sausage roll and packet of crisps!!! All he had to do was ask. ☺

Crown Court

Monday 24 June was the date set for Guildford Crown Court and I elected to give my evidence by video link from Cardiff Crown Court. My sisters who were called as witnesses gave theirs in Guildford. In Cardiff, we sat in a room looking at a TV and had a talk with the CPS about procedures and protocol and what will be asked of me. CPS did not question me as they thought that the recorded interview, I made was powerful enough and this was played to the jury in a closed court. I know the defence have their job to do and when questioned by him next to nothing was mentioned about the abuse, I suffered at the hands of the defendant. I had to answer questions about my childhood etc. The only time he asked me about the four occasions was that after having a bath with him and then my mother would then dry me in the bedroom…load of bollox.

During the case, I learnt that Twat had abused C in a shed and also had child pornography on a laptop which C had seen and he tried to say that nothing had happened. He also tried to blackmail C and his wife was involved. This was said in court but he had got rid of the laptop by the time he was questioned about C. From what I learned after the verdict was that he lied his arse off in court saying he loved his son and bullshitted his way through the whole case. I was totally gobsmacked at that.

There were a couple of times in Guildford that the case was paused as Susan was in the public gallery and said a few choice words directed at the twat. After eight days the jury were sent out and after two days came back with a verdict. What the Jury did not know was that on the first day they were out the twat went home to Portsmouth and attempted suicide with his wife!!! Is this the mind of a not guilty person? He spent the night in an MH unit being assessed. On the next day the police had to go and collect him and take him to court for the verdict which was announced while he was on his way…Not Guilty. We were all dismayed as to how and why they came to that decision as he DID abuse me as a child. There is nothing else I can do, so I decided to write about my childhood and name him. He has lost ALL of his family on our side as nobody believed a word he said in court but the jury. I always maintain that it was a difficult case to prove as it was historical sex abuse but the CPS and my family certainly believed that it happened. I don't know what the jury thought or how they came to that decision but they got it wrong in my case. I can't answer for C but I'm 99.9% certain he abused her.

I feel now that after 50 years of carrying a burden and that I still get flashbacks, I can feel at ease as the subject is out there and I was a victim. To keep something like this in your head for 50 years certainly takes its toll on a person. The last four years have really been tough not just on me but my immediate family as they have had to listen to and watch me on a steady downward spiral. I am at the stage now where I have let it all out and although relieved of talking of it, in a way it brings it back to the surface as with all memory it will always be there. In life when you experience something as traumatic as what I went through as an 11-year-old boy you learn to block it out but it still surfaces when I see incidents on the news or read in the papers of Paedophiles.

There is help out there for anybody who has had the same experience and I know it is a big step to take but you have to let it out, I kept it hidden away for 50 years and it not only affected me when I told the police about it but also my family. I did tell my wife many years ago the something had happened to me as a child but never elaborated; now she has had to live my nightmares and my ups and downs.

I have never been one for showing my emotion and since I revealed the secret, I have not stopped crying at the thoughts of what I suffered at the hands of someone who brought me into this world. It really has been a roller coaster of ups and downs in the last few years. It will never go away but knowing that I don't have to carry this burden anymore makes it a bit easier.

Thank you for taking the time to read my life story. I can be contacted on eggy.hepburn36@yahoo.com

My heartfelt thanks to the police at Guildford SUI (Sean and Jason) who took the initial report and believed what they heard, the Crown Prosecution Service also for believing in me and pursuing the paedophile that abused me and finally ALL of my family for listening and understanding what I went through as a child. It was a rough journey and the twat is no longer part of our family. (He has never been part of mine), there will not be a tear shed from me when he departs this earth.

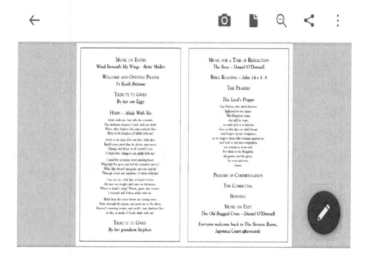

The service for Mum

Amazing what you see when attending the Army v Navy Rugby (Babcock Trophy) on the way to Twickenham.

Gwenny

HMS Arethusa Divisions on the Jetty in Singapore 1979. (Back row, right hand corner)

HMS Arethusa F38 1978–1981

Hms Invincible Beach Banyan in Antigua (I'm holding the flag)

Diego Garcia

HMS Invincible R05 1983–1986

HMS Nubian F131 1974–1977

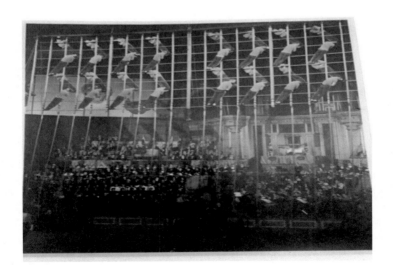

1982 Royal Navy Display Team (bottom row 4th from Right)
Practice session Royal Albert Hall

1988 British Forces Broadcasting Service

1992 Royal Overseas Police Officer Diego Garcia

5ES Mess, HMS Invincible with Royal Marines Commandos

1982 Royal Navy Display Team Portsmouth Guildhall Square.